BREAKAWAY

The Secret to Limitless Selling Success
Heroic Service

Tim Phillips

READERS PRAISE

"This is a great book for individuals involved in professional services that have not received formal sales training. The book provides the author's insight regarding four pillars for relationship-based, selling success, each providing realistic tactics that can be immediately put into daily practice. Every chapter is sprinkled with wisdom statements for the reader to dwell upon with the goal of shifting their life into one based on cause and purpose rather than being victimized by life's circumstances. I enjoyed reading this concise personable book and when finished, I put it down feeling BREAKAWAY was well worth the money. I am looking forward to the next one from Tim Phillips!"

★★★★★- Amazon Reader Review

"Unlike most motivational and sales authors today, the author of "BREAKAWAY" doesn't feel the need to say in 100 words what can be said in 10. In that spirit I will briefly say that this book is straightforward, enjoyable to read, and leaves the reader better off for having invested the time to read it. It's not a traditional sales book. It doesn't have countless chapters filled with methodologies and consulting schlock. Instead, this book offers tried and true lessons (referred to as pillars) that anyone should follow in order to provide the heroic service that will result in success both in sales and life."

★★★★★- Kindle Reader Review

"People don't want to be "sold", people don't want your stories, they value outstanding service. This is a thoughtful and concise guide of how to identify and provide true value to everyone in your circle of influence. If you want a life, run a business or lead a team where impact outsizes effort this is your instruction manual."

★★★★★- Amazon Reader Review

"With simplicity, candor, real world expertise, and thought provoking concepts and ideas Tim encapsulates in his first of four books the essence of what it takes to be a true service oriented professional. Having had the pleasure of being the recipient of Tim's expertise in companies that I have ran, I can tell you that the conceptual contents of this book truly work in real life and business situations. This is a must read for any business professional or entrepreneur who wishes to exponentially elevate his business sense, acumen, and service level."

★★★★★- - Kindle Reader Review

BREAKAWAY

The Secret to Limitless Selling Success
Heroic Service

Tim Phillips

ISBN: 978-0692577929

CONTENTS

PREFACE

Welcome! You may be opening this book in a bookstore or on an electronic reading device. Perhaps it was given to you as a gift or as suggested reading from a friend, colleague or family member. And now you're skimming through the preface to decide if the enjoyment and wisdom to be gained reading it is worthy of investing your most precious asset: time. I give you my personal pledge: it is. Read on.

This book is as much about the journey as it is the destination. Both the journey and the ultimate destination are yours. My intent is to serve as your guide in this journey. To accelerate reaching your defined personal destination in the most direct path possible through the benefit of my personal experience and wisdom gained in a thirty-five-year career of selling professional services. A career as a quota-carrying salesman that led into executive sales leadership and successful entrepreneurship, and now into serving as a consultant and counselor to leaders in some of the world's most dynamic enterprises.

My personal goal and psychic compensation is to empower you in lighting the fire of desire and fueling the drive to maximize your professional potential with a proven, defined system you can immediately implement to achieve limitless success — as you define it.

The system, concepts and techniques shared in the following pages are not exclusive to business, but have direct application for anyone wanting to achieve happiness and limitless success in creating a rich, rewarding and exceptional life few dare to dream of living.

Life is not a trial run. You have only one shot to make it all you want, with all the rewards, accomplishments and benefits earned through serving others.

My sincere desire in writing this book is to provide you with the means to achieve your most unimaginable dreams and create a life of immeasurable joy and fulfillment.

My commitment as your guide on this journey of self-discovery and action is to share with you the secrets I have received from countless guides, counselors, mentors and friends. These secrets and understandings were earned through wonderfully challenging experiences, and in more than a few cases, I share painful life lessons with you to accelerate your climb on the earning curve in pursuit of achieving your personal vision of limitless success.

Again, welcome – and remember as we move forward together, it is both the journey and the destination of achieving limitless success that contain the joy and the reward.

INTRODUCTION

There is beauty and elegance in simplicity — and if that belief makes me a simple man, I'm guilty as charged. There is also clarity in brevity; my approach and tone are honest and to-the-point. Your personal success is directly tied to your ability to understand and utilize the foundational principles of *heroic service* presented in the following pages.

In this book you will discover and understand the specifics of the heroic service system — the who, what, where, when, why and how of this system will empower you to achieve your personal limitless success. The use of specific experiences, models and examples will serve to reinforce the foundational concepts and support the heroic service pillars.

Although the examples in this book are of a professional nature, the concepts and techniques presented are easily adapted and applied in defining, engaging in, and maximizing the value of any human relationship.

You will also find statements throughout the book noted as **Wisdom**. These are universal points and mental placeholders created for you to "break away" from the herd through daily use. These wisdoms are summarized at the end of the book.

The key to unlocking your limitless personal success is not found in simply reading the words on the following pages. Limitless success requires having the courage to step out of your current comfort zone, built from unfounded doubts, beliefs and opinions reinforced through negative experiences and, all too often, unwarranted self-criticism.

You have the power to transform your life and to make the unimaginable reality. That liberating power is in the action that breaks the chains of old habits fastening us to the status quo raft, so that we are no longer tossed along the river of life.

The choice is yours: embrace the power of living life in a state of cause and purpose, or be swept in the current of victims of circumstance.

Choose life, choose action, and most of all, choose the freedom found in limitless success through liberating service to others. Go for it!

CHAPTER I:

HEROIC SERVICE

I can hear you saying, "What in the world is this heroic service?" The *what* is simple.

> ✎ **Wisdom: Limitless success is achieved through serving others heroically.**

This unique tenet of belief, defined as *heroic service*, is the foundation upon which my system of achieving limitless success is attained. The beauty of this approach is in the elegance of its simplicity.

We, both as individuals and as a society, have lost our way in understanding what words really mean in our modern era. It is critically important to have a clear definition and understanding of terms and how they will be applied going forward.

Service

First is the term *service*. Misuse and overuse of the word has resulted in dilution of what service truly is, as we tend to quickly jump to meaningless descriptive qualifiers like *good*, *fair* or *bad*. Not to mention the endless list of the hollow and valueless *un-* words — *unequaled, unimaginable, unparalleled*. Or, we fall prey to the advertising hyperbole of *premium*, *best in class*, *red carpet, exceptional, world class, gold key* or *royal.* The list of vacuous adjectives goes on forever in every new marketing pitch, ad campaign, and promotion du jour.

Whether you provide a product, a product with a service, or a purely intangible and invisible service, the key to limitless success is to first gain a clear understanding of what service is, where it starts, and its intended purpose.

Service, very simply, is helping someone do something they cannot, or choose not, to do for themselves. End of story. A word of caution: Simple should never be confused with easy.

More important than what service *is*, is knowing and understanding the perspective and manner in which the person, entity or enterprise provides service to another. Or, put in simple terms, the *by whom*, the *for whom* and the *how* service is to be given.

> ◈ **Wisdom: Attaining limitless success is achieved through intentionally adopting and living the true persona of the ultimate service provider:** *the servant.*

"Whoa! Hold it right there!" I can hear you saying, "I'm OK with helping people and providing great service, but I am <u>not</u> going to be a servant to anyone. I've worked too long, too hard, and am too smart to be anyone's servant."

Fear not! It's OK — you're not alone. This immediate reaction to the word *servant* is almost universally visceral. However, it is predicated upon ignorance in understanding what *servant* truly means and the incredible power it holds.

Words Have Meanings

Do not confuse the word *servant* with *subservient*. A servant is a person who intentionally and willingly helps another person do something they cannot or choose not to do on their own.

The servant is more powerful than the person being served. It is the spirit of service from which this great concept is derived: earning in exchange for a service. The exchange of service-based value is the true driver for all enterprise and economic endeavor.

On the other hand, *subservient* refers to a position of submission resulting in one person or entity having less power than another. That loss of power may be voluntary, as in the case of a servant, or involuntary, or even with a loss of personal freedom at the extreme, as in slavery. A servant should never be confused with a slave.

Servants earn! And in many cases, they earn huge sums of money and consideration from those they serve, while a slave is reliant upon a master to *give* him what he needs — food, shelter, etc. — so he can produce more value, not for himself, but for the master.

🐍 **Wisdom: The servant <u>earns</u> from a position of power, while the slave <u>is given</u> from a position of submission.**

Servants possess greater power than those they serve because the servant's power is in his ability, desire, intent and action to help the one being served.

<u>Heroic Service</u>

What is the ultimate level of service? Simple: heroic.

Let's turn our attention to the true meaning of the word *hero*, and how when used as an adjective to describe a manner of service — heroic — it becomes the ultimate level of service performance.

🐍 **Wisdom: The hero (or heroes) is an individual (or group) who performs a service for another in a manner establishing the measure by which all others are measured.**

Again, words have meaning. Unfortunately, words become blurred or misunderstood through ignorance or willful misapplication designed to mislead.

Take, for example, the words *hero* and *celebrity*. They are not synonymous. The celebrity is an individual that generates and garners notoriety with or without the provision of any service. They can, in fact, be famous or infamous, and may even earn large sums of money. Ken Lay, Jane Fonda, Tiger Woods, Bernie Madoff, Oprah and Roger Clemens are all celebrities.

A hero can be a celebrity. However, not all celebrities are heroes. And sadly, in today's mass media, sound-bite world, celebrities have greater acclaim than heroes. The hero, though, is the individual of whom legends are made and then grow over time, whereas, in most cases, the celebrity is but a brief, shining flash-in-the-pan with fifteen minutes of fame. Heroes that were also celebrities during life but have stood the test of time are Aristotle, Homer, Moses, Washington, Lincoln, Churchill, Houston, Kennedy, Ghandi and Dr. King.

If it is the hero's performance of service that establishes the standard by which all others (our peers, competitors and rivals) are measured, then the key for our individual limitless success should be the intentional performance of service as a hero in the eyes of those we serve.

> ❧ **Wisdom: Heroes endure from generation to generation, while celebrities fade and are soon forgotten.**

Powerfully Revealing Questions

A very telling combo-question to ask is, "Who are your heroes, and why?"

The answers to this question provides a tremendous amount of insight into our core beliefs, principles and values, and gives us a guide to how we might best emulate the performance characteristics of our heroes to position ourselves in like company.

Don't believe me? Try this simple experiment:
- ? Write down three names of your heroes.
- ? Next to each name, complete this statement: "What I admire most about ___ is . . ."

For most people, this list changes over time as we age, grow, and hopefully gain wisdom.

Now, for the really bold and fearless, here's another interesting experiment:
- ? Ask your children to do the same. Their heroes and reasons will blow you away!

You will quickly learn the difference between the perception and definition of heroes and celebrities. Ready to really push the envelope? Ask the questions of your spouse, or better yet, your boss! All of the concepts presented can be applied to both your professional network and your personal relationships.

As you become more comfortable asking these questions, you'll start to have a lot of fun learning about people through the answers and opinions they share. It's perfectly OK to have fun, and even laugh, along the path of experience we walk in the journey of life. In fact, all of my heroes have a great sense of humor while living and loving life to its fullest. So go for it!

From a business development and sales perspective, we all know the old adage that there is no better advertising than word-of-mouth from our own happy customers. Performing at a heroic level not only recognizes this marketing axiom, but takes it to the highest level, from generally positive referrals to clients proactively proclaiming your heroic performance to their entire circle of influence with comments like, "Man, I can't tell you what a great job Carl over at XYZ did for us! He truly saved us from a disaster we never saw coming. He's my hero."

The Worthiness of Pursuing Heroic Service

Heroic service is worthy of pursuit for one simple reason: Regardless of how much time, energy, effort, or passion a person or organization invests in any endeavor, the ultimate outcome can never be perfect. It can be great, but it's impossible to be perfect. However, that is not to say we should ever yield in our ongoing pursuit of perfection, as the pursuit itself results in excellence, the standard by which all others are measured. It is the pursuit of perfection that results in the creation of a hero (or heroic organization) in the eyes of a client, peer, superior or subordinate.

☙ Wisdom: Perfection is unattainable. Nevertheless, it is a worthy pursuit, as it results in excellence.

The pursuit of excellence through heroic service to others has another major benefit: the prevention of stagnation, complacency, or in the worst case, obsolescence or insignificance.

Heroic service to others should be the starting vision, initial action, and continuous touchstone for critical self-evaluation in assessing performance individually and collectively. Heroic service goes beyond quality, although quality is a component. Heroic service is the intentional action of giving oneself in going above and beyond the norm to help others achieve their vision of ultimate success. In striving to make others successful, we in turn achieve success.

How to Know When Heroic Service Success is Achieved

As management guru Stephen Covey teaches, before beginning any journey or venture, start with a clearly defined end or destination in mind. Without a defined end, it is impossible to know if that end is achieved.

Achieving heroic service is beautiful in its simplicity; people will say, "You're my hero," and you'll know you've succeeded.

And not necessarily figuratively, in some form of interpretation of a client satisfaction survey. Quite literally, people will say, or better yet, write, "You're my hero." You cannot imagine how motivating, empowering and energizing it is to hear someone say those three magic words. Moreover, you will know with complete and absolutely certainty that you have hit the desired mark of performance by which all others will be measured going forward: "You're my hero."

STOP! Take a minute and let that sink in.

Think about what it would mean if you, along with every employee in your company, in every action they took to serve a client need, were focused intentionally in making that person say:

"Wow! That's awesome, you're my hero."

"I can't imagine how we would've ever met that deadline without you. You're my hero."

"I'll never be able to repay you. We were upside down and in the ditch, and you did whatever it took to get us back on track. You're my hero."

These are but just three real examples of actual statements made by my clients, in relationships I established, grew and nurtured on a daily basis through the practice of heroic service. In addition, these three clients proactively made introductions to their friends, which led to further relationships served, sustained and grown. Referral relationships produce countless dollars in professional service fees without you spending a dime on advertising or promotion.

Referrals vs. References

There is a huge difference between a reference and a referral, and an even greater difference between a good provider of quality service at a fair price and a hero that delivers services viewed as incomparable and priceless. Read on for further expansion of this point.

🐦 **Wisdom: Referrals are free. References must be asked for.**

CHAPTER II:

THE THREE KEYS TO HEROIC SERVICE

The three key critical success factors in providing service and performing in a heroic manner are desire, intent and action.

Heroic service is not for everyone. And yes, it requires diligence, perseverance and plain old hard work to achieve. Even if in reading this book, the concept is appealing, logical and believable enough that you decide to become a heroic service provider, but do not *act* on that decision, you will absolutely fail. Wow! That's a shot in the arm. Why? You will fail because you didn't commit to all three of the critical success factors. Even with two out of three, you will fall short of the desired performance; there are no shortcuts. Just like a three-legged stool, without any one leg, the stool falls over.

𝔖 Wisdom: The Three Keys of Heroic Service Success: Desire, Intent, and Action

Desire – Starts in the head, with conscious thought through a logical process of understanding the requirements, risks and rewards in pursuing a defined path of action. Boiled down to its essence, desire is making the decision, "I want to."

Intent – Deepens the desire in the heart. Intent is taking a logical desire and defining and committing the requisite focus, resources (human, capital, training and time) and discipline to achieve the desired end. Intent is manifested in statements that say, "I will."

Action – Is the force multiplier of hands moving forward intentionally to achieve the desired end. Action requires the confidence and courage to persevere even if the first tries miss their mark. Actions are observable and speak louder than words, but can also be evidenced by comments such as, "I am."

Desire – "I Want" – The Head – Deciding

Intent – "I Will" – The Heart – Committing

Action – "I Am" – The Hands – Doing

From personal experience in working with thousands of people, I've found 90 percent of people have desire and 50 percent are intentional, but less than 10 percent will take action. Hence, the majority of the world languishes in silent desperation and meager existence. That's why there are so few heroes. Many want, dream, envision and hope, but only a bold few act.

The achievement of the ultimate rewards of sustainable client-for-life relationships — impenetrable by competition, never questioning the investment required, and continuously providing proactive relationship referrals as a result of the servant's heroic service — is only possible through the application of the head, heart and hands of desire, intent and action.

Not up for the challenge? It's OK. Most aren't. Pass this book to a willing friend or colleague.

My experience has shown that of these three critical ingredients for success, action is most often the one lacking, resulting in sub-optimal performance and/or failure. It is far better to act with less-than-perfect design than to not act at all, as most people will see, recognize and even reward your desire and intent in even a less-than-perfect action.

We also know that the evil, performance-stunting twin of inaction is procrastination. Many people and organizations have a genuine and committed desire and intent to become heroic in the eyes of their clients, but through engrained behaviors, experience-based traditions, misaligned reward systems, or plain outright fear, they fail to act and thus never achieve their full potential as heroic service providers.

> **Wisdom: Do something. Anything. Even doing something poorly is more rewarding than doing nothing at all.**

Limitless Success

At this point, you've noticed that the term *limitless success* is used extensively throughout this book. As with everything else in this book, its usage is intentional. It is important that you understand what limitless success is and how powerful a motivating force it can be in your life.

Success and failure are often defined and gauged in some form of tangible quantitative measure or demonstrable evidence. We are conditioned to view events in terms of success and failure. These two opposite states in our lives serve as motivating stimuli for our action or inaction.

We are not going to take the off-ramp into a study of the foundations of behavioral psychology, neuro-linguistic programming, or the myriad of faiths and religions known to mankind. Nor will we delve into the yin and yang of heaven and hell in pursuit of self-actualization.

Instead, simply stated, we are all, to varying degrees, constrained by a self-imposed set of beliefs and behaviors, almost all of which are rooted in fear fed by conventional wisdom, naysayers, fear-mongers and the little people leading desperate lives ruled by fear and self-loathing.

I believe success is truly limitless. Success is one of the few things we are truly capable of defining, refining, pursuing and achieving, both individually and collectively. One major shortcoming we have in pursuing and achieving success, limitless or otherwise, is that we fail to take the first action of defining it.

Start with desire. Define your desire with thought, discernment and judgment while asking the pivotal intentional question, *why*?

This is the one case where action can be the enemy of desire and intent, as we become mired in habits, rituals and programmed paths of action in the pursuit of success (or, more often, the avoidance of failure), a success that is undefined or ill-defined, at best. And sadly, in many cases, our image of success has been defined by someone else, and we have unconsciously adopted it as our own. The billions of advertising dollars annually spent on Madison Avenue confirm this reality.

Now that you possess this awareness, the call to action for you is to individually, and in collaboration with your family and organizational peers, craft and define a statement of limitless success complete with all the specific characteristics and attributes of what it looks and feels like, and most importantly, how you will know you've achieved it.

One of the easiest ways to start this dialogue with yourself or others is to ask the question, "In a perfect world with no limitations, how would you define success, and how would you know when you achieve it?" Then define, to the highest degree of specificity possible, the quantifiable measures that will serve as the success achievement indicators.

Be candid, and make sure you're setting realistic expectations based upon your physical limitations. I will never be able to dunk a basketball on a 10-foot goal, so defining my success as "being a pro NBA player" is unrealistic. Find the balance, and be true to yourself, not to the imposed beliefs of others. Be sure to **put your**

definition in writing, but don't carve it in stone, or it might become your epitaph.

Congratulations! You've just achieved the most difficult step in the process: the definition of your limitless success, complete with defined goals.

The final step is much easier. Lay out the goals on a timeline (or better yet, an actual calendar) with deadlines. Now list the actions required to achieve the goals on the timeline alongside a deadline for each action and the person responsible for performing the action. Voila! You have just completed your limitless success strategic plan.

The Conundrum

Now, here's both the problem and value in planning. First, a goal without a deadline is nothing more than a dream. Second, a plan not in writing is nothing more than spitballing, which results in recriminations and regrets in the form of "woulda, shoulda, coulda."

WARNING: Be on guard, and do not allow the planning process to become the definition of success. In other words, do not waste your most precious and truly non-renewable resource — TIME — in the consuming jaws of analysis paralysis. Any great plan immediately changes once the first shot is fired. Start taking action immediately, then modify the plan as results are achieved.

Bottom line: Do it now. Do something, anything, but do it now. There is little more powerful in this world — as proven by history, especially when it comes to heroic service performance — as first-mover advantage. Do it now!

Pouring the Foundation: The Power of Words

There are over 400,000 four-letter words in the English language. Interestingly, many are polar opposites: love/hate, give/take, push/pull, lift/drop, etc. Many of these we use interchangeably, and often incorrectly, with little or no thought.

Words are extremely powerful tools, especially the four-letter ones, and should be used intentionally, thoughtfully and with sound judgment. Much like driving a car or using a chainsaw, tools used in a cavalier way can have extreme and unintended consequences.

Sadly, many people use words without much care or discernment. Call this "language laziness," and when it comes to establishing, building and maintaining relationships, it will get you killed.

Words have defined, discrete meanings, as we find in the dictionary. Study and learn them, and strive to use them with precision and appropriateness. But, more importantly, recognize that the words we use have a deeper emotional power we sometimes fail to take into account.

It is essential that we understand the foundational principle of the power of language in heroic service, as it is this foundation upon which we will erect the four pillars of heroic service success.

Four Pillars of Heroic Service Success

We've defined and committed to our heroic service plan for limitless success, and we've briefly discussed the power of words in our foundation for heroic service. Let's now turn to the four specific action steps, the pillars upon which heroic service is built.

CHAPTER III:

THE FIRST PILLAR

<u>Always Give Value First to Earn More</u>

The first of the four pillars draws its strength from the recognition of the difference between two key four-letter words. If you take but one concept from this reading, this one alone will serve you well in achieving your goal of becoming a hero in the eyes of all you serve. It is the understanding of the differences between two related, but often misunderstood, words: *give* and *earn*.

This is not only a key pillar — it's the keystone of heroic service. Of the four pillars, this one is most paradoxical and counter-intuitive. As such, it's difficult for most people to get their heads around it and embrace it intentionally with action.

I promise that if you can master the principle of this pillar and leverage its power, you will succeed in virtually every facet of every relationship in your life, beyond your wildest imagination.

Throughout my career, I have tracked and calculated that the amount of success you will earn in any relationship is usually a minimum multiple of 10 times the amount you give away.

In other words, the more you give away, the more you will earn, at an ever-increasing rate.

Having spent my entire career in sales, I only wish someone would have clued me in to this fact thirty-five years ago. It is the closest thing I have found to approximate the natural law of relationships, akin to the laws of physics or nature.

The problem is that most people, including myself, really don't take the time to consider the differences between the words *earn* and *give*, let alone the words *give* and *take*. We think about it even less when using them in the form of actions — earning vs. giving vs. taking.

  🦢 **Wisdom: We must be willing to fearlessly give to earn without considering what's in it for us.**

Stop! Re-read that sentence and let it sink in for a minute. I can hear you now. "Oh boy, is this guy nuts! If I give my product or services away, I will rapidly be out of business, with no clothes on my back or food on my table. You gotta be kidding me!"

Please don't consider me Pollyanna-ish, naive or stupid. Test me. Where do you think the concept of the "free sample" is rooted, and why? Marketers and salesmen have recognized this pillar principle since the dawn of time. It's in everything from the car test drive and the new product sample in the grocery store, to the sign-up for the free 30-day trial with your credit card. The key is in what you **choose** to give away.

Let me share with you a true story of this pillar in practice. I had been working unsuccessfully for several weeks to schedule a meeting with the VP of Sales of the largest professional employer organization (PEO) in the U.S. We'll call him Marty.

Through chance, I received an email invitation from a client/friend (I view all clients as friends) and saw that Marty was scheduled to speak at a breakfast forum hosted by the Houston Technology Center on selling professional services. I registered, attended and, at the conclusion, made my way forward to introduce myself to Marty and exchange business cards. I kept our talk short and to-the-point, as there's nothing worse than the post-session conversation monopolist — please don't ever be one. I told Marty I would like to visit with him further, as I felt our thoughts were aligned in that selling is about helping other people get what they want, not just what they need. This entire initial meeting took no longer than one minute.

Marty gave me an hour on his calendar; we'd meet in two weeks. The purpose of this meeting was what most would call an initial "meet and greet." I prefer to call them "show up and serve," as I went to see if there were any areas where I could be of service, and to determine if Marty and his company's services would be a good fit as a client.

Now, here's where the power of always giving value first to earn more comes into play. I came prepared, as I do for all meetings, with the names of four of my clients

I felt would be good candidates for Marty's organization and had a need for their services. We had a great visit, as both of us were masters of consultative questioning skills. (We'll hit those later.)

You will come to experience and appreciate the joy of sharing time with other consultative communication practitioners (which all truly great sales pros are). In the last fifteen minutes of our scheduled hour, I shared with Marty my belief in the first pillar of heroic service, and that I had come prepared with the names of four clients. I asked for the name of his local salesperson with whom I could share this information. Guess what? Our hour expanded by thirty minutes.

First, Marty, again being a sales pro, asked me qualifying questions about the client companies — size, location, industry, ownership, etc. Then he whirled in his chair to his computer and gave me not just one name, but the names and contact numbers for four of his field sales representatives. I thanked him for his time and told him that as a next step, I would create some ideas about how I might be of service to his firm in light of their rapid growth, resource constraints and performance objectives.

After the meeting, I contacted Marty's four sales reps and tracked my experiences and results in dealing with each sales rep as they questioned me and began to contact, qualify and meet with my clients.

I tracked and logged everything from timeliness and quality of responsiveness to follow-through with my clients. It took about three weeks for all four of the reps to make it through the process. During this time, I did not call Marty or his Executive Assistant to schedule our next meeting. Again, it is **important to earn the opportunity to demonstrate value and not ask for it to be given**. I would earn the next appointment with Marty through tangible results and findings.

Rather than calling or emailing to schedule a meeting, I prepared a brief but comprehensive email outlining the experiences of my interactions and follow-throughs with the four sales reps, along with a high-level assessment of their strengths to build upon and weaknesses to improve. In closing, I asked if he might have some time on his calendar to discuss some ideas I had formulated not only from this experience, but also from our first meeting.

Do you think I got the meeting? Oddly enough, I didn't receive an email back from Marty! But I was copied on an email from him forwarding my note to his Executive Assistant, requesting that she coordinate calendars for me to meet with Marty as his guest at Redstone Country Club for lunch and golf, and then to attend the Houston Astros game that evening in the company box to meet some of his clients and sales team members.

The happy ending to this story is that two of the four referrals I'd provided in that initial "show up and serve" meeting actually became clients of Marty's PEO. They have been thrilled with the value and the service, and I moved up another notch on the always-trying-to-help hero scale. At the same time, Marty and I forged a rewarding and mutually beneficial professional relationship and friendship.

Most people I have observed floundering and continuously failing in life and relationships are unwilling to give to earn, and are instead focused on someone giving them something, or worse, on taking business from a "sucker." These people struggle in misery with a life's-not-fair mindset as they desperately grovel in the pit of the relationship-challenged.

Whenever you want to establish a new relationship or deepen an existing one, do so intentionally with the heart of a proactive giver trusting in the power of the first pillar. Over time, you will earn more than you give. Don't worry about the "takers." The takers take care of themselves, and we'll address how to discover them early on a little later.

🔊 **Wisdom: Give a little to earn a lot.**

Summary of First Pillar: Always Give First to Earn More

- The amount of success you earn in any relationship is usually a minimum multiple of 10 times the amount you give away.
- We must be willing to fearlessly give to earn without considering what's in it for us.
- Seek to earn, <u>don't</u> ask to be given.
- Give a little – earn a lot.

CHAPTER IV:

THE SECOND PILLAR

Practice the Platinum Rule

This second pillar took me many years to discover and understand. In fact, truth be told, it wasn't revealed to me until very recently through a personal experience I will never be able to repay. But once I "got it" and intentionally put the pillar into practice, it became a force multiplier unlike any other pillar.

I was taught at an early age the Golden Rule: "Do unto others as you would have them do unto you." I even thought I did a fairly good job of practicing it in most relationships.

However, it is interesting to note that the Golden Rule focuses on you, the doer. What if the recipient wants to be "done unto" in a manner different than I would?

Before I share with you the definition of the Platinum Rule and how it differs from the Golden Rule, I'd like to share how I discovered it. I believe the path of discovery is of immense value.

In 2004, I had the great fortune to be a civilian volunteer for a company of U.S. Marines deployed to Iraq. One of my personal heroes was a member of this company: my younger brother, Captain Matthew Phillips.

As part of his duty, upon returning from Iraq after having been wounded in Fallujah, Matthew served as a Casualty Assistant Call Officer (CACO). A CACO is a Marine officer responsible for the personal notification of a Marine's designated next of kin in the event a Marine is killed or mortally wounded in combat action. In addition, a CACO coordinates the return of the deceased Marine's remains, planning of the family funeral, command of the escort and burial details, presentation of the ceremonial flag draping the coffin, and all administration and processing of surviving family member death and insurance benefits.

A CACO keeps a dedicated cell phone with them at all times for the express use of being notified of a Marine killed in action. Upon receipt of such a call, a CACO arrives unannounced on the doorstep of a home to personally deliver the news of the loss to the Marine's family members, regardless of time of day, weather or location.

Now, I have had to personally deliver some very tough news in my life, but it is unimaginable to me how these Marine officers have the ability — all without special screening, personality profiling, communication or grief counseling skills assessment, and with minimal administrative training — are able to conduct such an emotionally wrenching mission.

And that's not even accounting for the unknown and unforeseen response of the family members receiving the news every service member's family dreads and prays will never come. Talk about true heroes.

The Platinum Rule was revealed to me in the answer to a very simple, direct question I asked Matthew: "How are you able to perform your duty, not knowing how people will react to such news?"

The true beauty of the answer was in its elegant simplicity: "I do it in the way I would want someone to do it for my wife, child, mother or father."

That made logical sense and fit within my understanding of the Golden Rule. But it was Matthew's next statement that completely caught me off-guard and opened my eyes to the true power of the heroic servant's Platinum Rule: "Then I try as quickly as I can to determine how they want me to engage with them. And I adapt my behavior to their desires."

Wham! When I heard those words, it was like all the tumblers in the combination lock of my mind fell into place, and a new door unlocked and opened. The power of the Platinum Rule was revealed.

❧ Wisdom: Do unto others as they want to be done unto.

It's not about me and my needs; it's all about them and their wants. I adapt to meet their wants, needs and desires to better serve them, and in so doing, I achieve my purpose. But I was burning to learn *how* to put this new principle into practice.

So, if the Platinum Rule is the standard for heroic service and is predicated upon treating people in the manner in which they want to be treated, rather than projecting how we would like to be treated in a particular situation...

How in the world can I know how someone else want to be treated?

Of course, most of us are not clairvoyant, so how can we know how people want to be treated? I posed the question directly to the steady Marine officer, who simply answered, *"I ask."* The great thing about Marines is, when you ask a question, you get a direct answer; I've never met a "flower-mouthed" Marine. Again, clarity in brevity is a unique gift.

Ask! Ask how they want to be treated, their preferred manner of communication, their deepest wants, needs, desires, aspirations and fears, so that we may serve them in the manner they desire to be served.

Sound too simple to be true?

Simple, YES. Easy, NO.

Not because it's difficult or mysterious, or we lack the intellectual capacity or communication skills. It's not easy because we have not been trained in or haven't practiced the proper questioning techniques to reveal the underlying desires of those we wish to serve.

The difficulty of applying the Platinum Rule is also the result of being behaviorally conditioned for immediate gratification in everything we do: "Give me the answer, I don't have the time or patience to earn it." As a result, most of us are poor questioners, and, rather than truly having an interest in genuine answers to bona-fide questions, we seek validation of a presupposed belief based upon what we want to get, our experiences, or our preconceived ideas.

In other words, we spend most of our time asking lame, thoughtless questions with little intention of truly hearing and understanding the answers to the questions we ask.

Consultative Questioning Skills to Engage the Platinum Rule

To maximize the value of the following consultative questioning skills, first decide you genuinely want to know the answer to your question from the other person's point of view. This can be much tougher than you think. But with practice comes mastery.

The most effective way to present these skills is by using a bit of verse from the famous nineteenth-century English poet Rudyard Kipling's poem, "The Elephant's Child":

> *"I keep six honest serving men*
> *They taught me all I knew*
> *Their names are what and where and when*
> *And how and why and who"*

This stanza provides us with the six words we need to find out anything about anyone at any time, by using them in the form of questions. However, not all six of the words, when used in the form of a question, are equal in their power. Yes, that's right, *power*. Words do, in fact, have varying degrees of power.

Power Hierarchy of Questions

Of the six, *what, where, when* and *who* are the least powerful when used in the form of a question. (Now I feel like we're playing *Jeopardy*.)

The 4 Ws

What, where, when and *who* are fact questions. They yield answers that are nouns — people, places, things and points in time. Look at these examples.

What is the title of this poem? "The Elephant's Child."
Who wrote this poem? Rudyard Kipling.
When did he write it? Nineteenth century.
Where did he write it? England.

We tend to naturally gravitate to these questions for one reason: Their answers tend to be short, factual and to-the-point, and require little sophistication of listening skills. These questions tell us what we want or think we need to know, rather than what the other person may really wish to be, or in some cases, is not telling us.

In the early 1960s there was a highly rated television show titled *Dragnet* about two Los Angeles police detectives, partners Joe Friday and Bill Gannon. Regardless of the situation, whether conducting an interview with a hysterical crime victim, mouthy thug, or long-winded witness, Friday's famous line was always delivered in the same deadpan tone, week after week, in every episode: "Just the facts, ma'am."

Friday had neither the time nor the inclination to hear anything other than the facts required to locate, arrest and convict the bad guy and keep the streets of Los Angeles safe another week. Joe Friday was, like most of us, in a hurry, and thus only interested in answers to surface-level questions, defaulting to *who, what, where* and *when*. Then again, he only had thirty minutes, including time for commercials.

The Power-Hitters

The two most powerful questions, by far, are *how* and *why*, because they cannot be easily answered with a fact!

How and *why* questions require some form of thought and opinion on the part of the person being asked. Most great interviewers and interrogators start with *how* and *why* questions. Then, if need be, you can use the fact yielding *what, where, when* and *who* to corroborate or refute the opinion-based *how* and *why* questions.

The absolute most powerful of the two is definitely ***why***.

Why? Great question! *Why* delivers the highest level of thought and, in many cases, emotionally driven opinions, beliefs, desires, wants, needs or fears. And, sadly, it is often the question we are too hesitant to ask.

Misguidedly, we may consider asking questions too challenging, deep, probing, or, in some cases, disrespectful or rude. However, when asked from a position of genuine desire to help another through the performance of the Platinum Rule, *why* will earn you the respect, confidence and even admiration of the person you serve.

Taking the Lead

Regardless of age, experience or expertise, most of us feel a momentary anxiety when speaking to or meeting another person for the first time. For me, this anxiety is rooted in my mother's admonition, "You have but one chance to make a first impression, and it lasts a lifetime."

In professional selling, we know this to be the gospel truth, as most people have determined in the first twenty seconds of meeting you whether they will engage with you or not. Fair, absolutely not. Truth, absolutely!

In recognition of this fact and in intentionally striving to heroically serve others, after initial introductions, open a business meeting with asking a *how* question in the present tense, reflecting their current point in time.

For example, in business, ask, "How's business?" If you're a health care provider, you can ask, "How's your health today?" The *how* question effectively does two things: First, it places the focus and importance on the other person, and, second, it encourages an opinion-based answer rather than a fact. Most importantly, it puts you in a position of leading in asking the questions with the intent to help the other person.

Notice that we do not ask, "How are you today?" or "How are you feeling?" or "How ya doin'?" These mundane questions evoke nothing more than an automaton response of "Good," "Fine," "Not so good," "I don't know," or "Great."

More important than the specific words we use in any question is projecting the underlying desire to genuinely know the answer. This is effectively done with appropriate tone and facial expressions, not with the brilliance of the words we choose.

Time: The Fourth Dimension

After establishing our role as the leader in asking the questions, use the power of the dimensions of time — past, present and future — by phrasing *how* questions through corresponding verb tenses. (I promise, no grammar lessons.) This allows us to gain an understanding and appreciation of where the other person has come from, where they are today, and where they aspire to be in the future.

Let me share with you an illustration of this technique, building upon the foregoing business example:

> "How's business?" (Present)
> "How was business?" (Past)
> "How would you like business to be?" (Future)

Oddly enough, of the three dimensions of time, most people focus on the past and present in the questions they ask, and rarely explore the future, instead preferring to project their preconceived beliefs or understandings on the other individual. One of the greatest techniques to set up the future tense *how* question is to use what I call the *runway phrase*: "So, in a perfect world. . . " This phrase removes all preconditions and allows the respondent to not only provide an opinion, but to engage their imagination in creating their vision of a future aspirational state, which you will help them achieve.

For example: "So tell me, Bill, in a perfect world, how would you envision your business?" In this example, using *perfect* and *envision* is intentional, as the words allow the person to create an image of what perfection would look like. Once the vision is stated, engage to help make the vision a reality.

Now let me show you how to use the power of combining *how* and *why*. *How* serves as a wedge that opens the door to the deeper-seated, and often unasked, *why*. When employed with a genuine sense of service to others, the following technique is the most powerful tool I have found. But before I share it, be forewarned that if its usage does not come from the heart in a genuine desire to help another, it will severely damage and, in all likelihood, kill a relationship.

Very simply, after having asked a *how* question (especially in aspiration-revealing future tense), pause and say nothing while looking at the other person, and then gently and genuinely ask *why*. The secret to this technique is not to utter another sound for however long it takes the person to reply. It may seem like an eternity, as you listen to your heart pound or the seconds ticking on your watch — and in all likelihood, it will feel that way until you become comfortable with the silence — but you absolutely must not speak. You're allowing the other person to think deeply and reflectively about their true underlying desires before answering your question.

Unfortunately, the majority of us fail to take the time to truly, thoughtfully consider the real *why* behind what we have, what we are or what we want to do. Don't be surprised if this question is often answered with a statement like, "You know, that's a really good question." Shut up and smile! You've just been paid a huge compliment and are rapidly transforming into sage and counselor. You've taken the first steps toward heroism in service to this person.

In conducting seminars and giving speeches at conferences, this is where some people begin to squirm in their seats, and the bold will say, "This sounds a little manipulative to me, and I'm not sure I feel comfortable asking people about their *how*s, much less their *why*s." This is a legitimate point predicated upon behavior patterns conditioned in us to extinguish the innate inquisitive nature we have in childhood, when we continually ask, "Why?"

Consultative communication techniques are not manipulative in and of themselves. They are proven effective in a wide array of situations, from casual conversation to formal interrogations, and are based upon open, honest communication with another human being. They do not use any form of deceit or coercion. Most importantly, they are used in our effort to help another person gain insight and understanding to the underlying *how*s and *why*s regarding what they have done, are doing, or aspire to do. And it is from and through that sense of service to others that we can rest easy and with a clear conscience.

> ⟠ **Wisdom: A clever man is known by the answers he gives. A wise man is known by the questions he asks.**

Take the time to craft and carefully practice an arsenal of *how* and *why* questions that evolve in depth and quality through application and experience.

Whole-Being Intentional Listening

The secret to being a truly heroic servant is taking the time to intentionally and consciously listen to the other person with all of your senses. The key is having the patience to maintain your bearing while affording the other person the time to reflect and respond. Whole-being intentional listening is doing just that: listening to others with all of your conscious senses, and even your unconscious ones (instincts or "gut"), to gain a full understanding of the other person's wants, needs, desires, dreams, aspirations and fears. At its base level, whole-being intentional listening means listening not only with your ears, but with your eyes. And not only to the words being said, but (sometimes more importantly) to the ones *not* being said.

I grew up in a household with not only a caring and loving mother and father, but a grandmother, as well. My grandmother was an incredible lady — an adventurous, athletic, outspoken business owner, a single mother of three, fearless and filled with more wisdom than I knew at the time. She had a repertoire of sayings she would draw upon in just the right circumstance to ensure a life lesson was made, even if it wasn't fully understood at the time. I would loquaciously present a case for extending my curfew or make a defense for violating the same, and my grandmother would patiently listen until I was all talked out, then simply say, "You were created with two ears and one mouth; use them proportionally." To this day, I think of that statement any time I step on my soapbox of self-righteous absorption.

I witness this truth being violated by aspiring salespeople who show up, pull the ripcord on the back of their heads and proceed to spew insignificant qualifications, facts, figures and even testimonials about their products and services, while never listening to the answer of the initial question asked, if one is even asked at all. The foundation of being a great communicator is not in one's eloquence of the spoken word, but in being an engaged and focused listener to gain an understanding of the other person's point of view.

What my grandmother was really saying was to spend one-third of our time speaking, as we have one mouth, and two-thirds of our time listening, as we have two ears. In terms of whole-being intentional listening, I have modified this 1:3 ratio of speaking-to-listening to a minimum of a 1:5, or 20 percent, ratio. Why? Quite simply, I believe I can actually "hear" more with my eyes through reading body language, facial expression and initial reactions to questions asked.

The real secret to being a heroic listener is to understand that if I have two eyes, two ears and one mouth, and use them proportionately, that yields a 1:5 or 20 percent ratio for speaking in my conversations and interviews. This is a new skill for most and will require a significant amount of practice. Use this new knowledge and hone it into an embedded, unconscious behavior by practicing it with everyone with whom you engage — coworkers, family, friends, everyone. You will rapidly become known as one of the most incredible conversationalists. Trust me, it works, so go for it!

<u>The Secret to Becoming a Whole-Being Intentional Listener</u>

The true secret to being a whole-being intentional listener is to use that precious 20 percent of time reserved for speaking to ask powerful thought- and opinion-provoking *how* and *why* questions.

The way I know I have achieved my goal of being a whole-being intentional listener is when the person with whom I am talking —in many cases, for extended periods of time — suddenly stops and, in mid-sentence, says, "Wow, I'm sorry, I've been doing all the talking here, and I don't really know much about you." That simple statement is music to our ears. There is little more appreciated by another human being than having their opinions heard and their feelings understood. You're on the path to heroic service. And your natural response to such a statement — and always with a wide smile — should be, "That's OK, we'll have plenty of time for that in the future, but right now I am really enjoying getting to know you and finding out how I might be able to deliver the greatest value in service to you." Immediately this should be followed with — I know you already beat me to the punch — asking another open-ended *how* and *why* question.

🐟 **Wisdom: People and enterprises that are externally focused on helping and serving others first will explode with success and growth, while those that focus internally on self will implode and limp along to ultimate failure.**

The Power of Presence

The last key element in effectively practicing the Platinum Rule is the increasingly undervalued yet incredible power of presence. In this age of email, text and instant messaging, conference calls, WebEx, cell phone, voicemail and automated call-forwarding systems to outsourced call centers, the power of physical presence in a meeting grows more valuable on a daily basis. So much so that the ability to conduct an effective face-to-face business meeting is becoming a lost art, yet remains the greatest competitive differentiator and the required venue for whole-being intentional listening. Bottom line, if you want to jump-start your business or establish any kind of personal relationship, you have to be in the same room with the other person at some point in time as the relationship evolves.

Out of sight leads to being out of the other person's mind. And what your absence effectively conveys is your neglect, your taking a relationship for granted and failing to meet with your clients on a regular basis. The fastest and surest way to kill a relationship is through neglect. No one likes being taken for granted, so they will proactively seek out and engage with someone who will at least listen.

Let me prove this to you with another personal example. I am married to the most beautiful woman in the world — my beloved Patricia. I know that is an incredibly bold statement, but nevertheless, it's true. As my grandmother would say, "Boy, I don't know how you did it, but you sure did marry up." Yes, I did.

Anyone who knows me will attest that every phone conversation I have with my bride, regardless of time, location or situation (even in times of stress, anger, or shall we say, less than marital bliss) ends with three simple, yet very important, words: "I love you."

Now many of you may think I am a hopeless romantic, which I may, in fact, be. Or that, given this crazy world we live in, we should never miss an opportunity to express our love and appreciation for our spouse, as it could be our last opportunity, which may be true, as well. But the real reason I always say "I love you" is much simpler: I am a hard-balled pragmatist, and I know for a fact, without any doubt, that I am truly married to the most beautiful woman in the world. And I know that if I do not tell my wife, "I love you," there are thousands of men out there who will. And I am never going to give them the chance. Could she find a smarter, wealthier, more handsome man than me? Absolutely! But I have full faith in her integrity, fidelity and honor, and I acknowledge those few of many wonderful character traits in simply saying, "I love you."

Your clients, or anyone with whom you are in a relationship, are dying to be acknowledged, appreciated and heard. Proactively look for and create opportunities in every situation to not only tell them, "I love you," but more importantly, to *show* you love them through your actions and performance. Remember, actions speak louder than words. Taking the initiative, making the time to meet with a person and engage all your whole-being listening skills, will rapidly raise you to hero status.

ဢ Wisdom: Showing up is half the battle.

If you can't meet with a client, increase the rate of contact using multiple sources until you have the next opportunity to meet. If you work independently or in a different location from your clients, leverage social media sites like LinkedIn and free video teleconferencing apps like Skype or Google Hangouts to connect with people. The ability to put eyes on a person and see their visual cues, along with hearing tone, volume and cadence, is invaluable in establishing initial rapport that grows into valuable relationships.

Let me share with you three practical ways (which should become habits) to constantly deliver and build value through non-personal contact.

First, answer and return all voicemails on the day they were received, regardless of the time, time zone, or how hopelessly weary you are. Even if you don't have the information requested, or the answer to a question left on your voicemail, return the call and let the client know. A hero never lets a person feel taken for granted. Returning calls has become a lost art, and it will separate you from the pack and set the standard by which all others are measured. The same holds true for returning other forms of communication — text, email, whatever. Just a simple response to the effect of, "Thanks for the note, I'll respond as soon as I have the requested information, which I anticipate will be on or before <u>date</u>."

Second, always be on the lookout for information that can help those whom you serve — articles, websites, blogs, and most of all, REFERRALS who might need their products or services. And do so with no expectation of being given the same. In other words, don't seek commissions for referrals; it is better to have a positive chit on the ledger that will come back multi-fold in lieu of a one-time finder's fee. You're investing in a long-term relationship.

And the third? I know you will roll your eyes and say, "No way, are you kidding? I don't have time to do this." But it may be the most important: Send a personal birthday card to everyone you serve. The card itself doesn't have to be expensive or fancy, but it must be handwritten and personally signed by you, or don't even waste your time with this technique. Why? Next to a person's name, which is always music to their ears, on their list of most important possessions is their special day — their birthday. I have never met anyone, regardless of their outward protest about celebrating birthdays, that doesn't enjoy their value as a human being acknowledged on but one day out of 365. Do you and your company spend lots of time, money and effort on sending impersonal holiday cards? So does everyone else. Re-channeling that investment into a birthday card program will differentiate you from the herd of lemmings. If you want, keep your holiday card program and supplement it with a birthday card program.

🐦 **Wisdom: It is the value of taking action, not the value of the act, which counts.**

Summary of Second Pillar: Practicing the Platinum Rule

- Do unto others as they would want to be done unto.

- Use your six honest serving men of consultative communication skills: *who, what, where, when, how* and *why.*
- Focus on the power of *how* and *why.*
- Be a whole-being listener.
- 80 percent listening, 20 percent speaking to ask *how* and *why* questions.
- Leverage the power of presence; showing up is half the battle.

CHAPTER V:

THE THIRD PILLAR

<u>"Do a Good Turn Daily"</u>

Busted! I did, in fact, borrow this phrase for the third pillar from the Boy Scouts. The reason again is the elegance of its simplicity, in terms of our ease of understanding and its ability to be transformed into intentional action. Actually, as all former Boy Scouts will readily recognize, "Do a Good Turn Daily" is the official Boy Scouts slogan.

<u>The Money Value of Time</u>

To fully understand this pillar, we first need to understand the *money value of time*. Elite, highest-producing sales pros understand this concept; it is the motivating focus for their actions and prioritizations.

Unlike the *time value of money* (the financial concept that a dollar today is worth more than a dollar tomorrow) that serves as the basis for all compounding interest, and discounting of future cash flows, to establish valuation criteria used in financial investment analysis. The money value of time recognizes that time is probably the only truly non-renewal natural resource. Time marches on, and no one can slow or speed it up, let alone stop or reverse it.

In recognizing that time stops for no man, we have to acknowledge that it is nearly impossible to manage time, as time is beyond our control. What we can do is choose in which activities we will invest our precious, finite amounts of time. It is the allocation and investment of time we control and decide, rather than time itself.

The principle of the money value of time, from a business perspective, is that we should invest our time in activities that yield the highest value for the amount of time invested. We have the power to choose if we invest our time in reading this book, watching a movie, writing a blog, meeting with a prospective client or performing a *good turn*.

> 🕉 **Wisdom: Focus on the money value of time, and invest your time wisely in activities that yield the highest reward for the time invested.**

It's Action That Counts

The power of this pillar is that it builds upon the prior two and moves them to the immediate in terms of time and frequency ("daily") by moving giving, serving and helping ("good turn") to the forefront of our conscious thoughts ("do"). The word *turn* in this case is synonymous with the word *act*. This pillar sharpens our focus on being intentional in "walking our talk" through daily action. It further calls us to personal accountability, in that we should make an honest assessment of ourselves throughout the course of any day by asking a very simple question: "What have I done today to help _____?" And then not close the day without doing at least one good turn.

ᗩ Wisdom: Better than the brilliant thought is bold action upon a less-than-perfect thought.

In the business world, one of the most powerful good turns is to provide your colleagues, current and prospective clients, vendors and channel partners with referrals. This is can be done easily, effectively and quickly using email. By providing an intro email to a business contact saying, "Bill, I want to introduce you to Laura with XYZ. Laura is one of my personal heroes, as she and her firm have helped us in reducing our spend on printing costs by 35%. I know you do almost twice the amount of printing we do, so she might be able to help you even more!" This simple email intro takes less than 5 minutes to write, but the multiplier effect is doubled because you've helped both parties with the good turn.

Another great example of a good turn is to email or retweet articles or blogs to people they may help. When others know you're thinking of them and investing the time to take action, there is a natural desire to balance the scale through reciprocation or, at a minimum, simple appreciation.

Join and participate in charities your clients or prospects are involved in, both individually and collectively. I engaged a new target client after reading that their CEO had just assumed the chairmanship of a local charity benefitting youth. I signed up, showed up and rolled up my sleeves with time, treasure and people. Not only did we engage in a long-term, rewarding professional relationship, but via the law of like attraction, we found two other clients through our active participation in the charity. Our team members also found a rich reward in the higher calling of serving those in need in their community. This form of a good turn is a win-win-win proposition – a business, personal and community win.

Building Your Reputation

Can you imagine what it feels like each and every day to know you have helped someone achieve something they could not have done without your help? Talk about building self-esteem! What will increase more than your personal self-esteem, and at an even greater rate, is your reputation. A reputation as someone who goes above and beyond in putting the interests, needs and desires of others first. A reputation for taking action without requiring payment or expecting reciprocity. A reputation as an action hero who establishes the standard by which all others are measured.

Just reading this book, understanding and agreeing with the ideas, concepts and techniques, and even possibly considering experimenting with or adopting some ideas, are all good and valuable. However, failing to act diminishes virtually all of the value of the time invested in reading and considering these ideas, as it is only through action that we can truly make change happen. Status quo is the enemy; it is to be challenged and defeated through action on a daily basis.

One great way to build your network reputation on a daily basis is to use the "Connections" function in LinkedIn. This function notifies you daily of everyone in your network with a birthday that day, as well as anyone who has received a promotion in their current organization or taken on a role in a new enterprise. By simply monitoring these Connections, you can send a brief, personalized birthday note, or congratulations on their new role. Three key things people love are seeing their name in writing, having their birth acknowledged, and a promotion or recognition in their profession. All three can be achieved in less than 15 minutes per day with the LinkedIn technology. The key is to *invest* those 15 minutes every day into your schedule. Beyond maintaining our ever-growing number of relationships, this tactic has proven a profitable technique in staying front-of-mind when a potential business need arises that we can satisfy. Remember: Out of sight, out of mind. At least once a year, on that person's most important day, you should be there to say, "Happy birthday."

Be the Change

In the famous words of Mahatma Gandhi, "Be the change you want to see in the world." The power of a human taking but one single action is terribly misunderstood and unappreciated. Every great thought, discovery, belief or movement in the world did not start with an idea (as we are often told), but with one person taking action on a single idea. Don't get me wrong, ideas and thoughts are the truly wondrous sparks of creativity. But I would trade a whole bushel of ideas for a single action upon one. Sadly, ideas not acted upon become delayed, stunted and in many cases lost forever. And so do lives.

Focus

Energy follows focus. Even though a laser can burn through steel, it is but a concentration of energy through focus. In the case of the laser, that's light energy. Isn't it odd that you cannot focus darkness? Darkness is but the absence of light, which is energy, and the absence of that energy cannot be focused.

The laser metaphor is directly applicable to people as well, both individually and collectively in organizations. The more diffused (lack of focus), the more confused (inefficient) and less effective (performance) we become in achieving our goal (success, however defined). Oftentimes this is evident in statements such as, "I'm not sure we're all on the same page," "We're not all in alignment," or, even more telling, "Why in the world are we doing this?"

The power of "Do a Good Turn Daily" is the focus it provides with its clarity and brevity. All we have to do is define for whom we will do a good turn daily. The key lies in first being intentional in doing a beneficial act for someone each day, and then, most importantly, doing it! Keep it simple, and make an honest assessment during the day, asking yourself, "What have I done today to help _____?" Haven't done anything? Then do it now.

🏵 **Wisdom: Thoughts, ideas and words without acts and deeds are but dust in the wind.**

Summary of Third Pillar: Do a Good Turn Daily

- The money value of time – "Invest in activities that yield the highest return"
- It's action that counts — "What have I done today to help?"
- Reputation — Action sets the standard by which all others are measured.
- Be the change — It just takes one you.
- Focus — Energy follows focus. Be the laser.

CHAPTER VI:

THE FOURTH PILLAR

<u>Forgive and Forget</u>

This pillar will help you maintain your bearing at all times and allow you to serve others heroically, even when faced with the inevitable disappointment of discovering that those you serve are, at best, imperfect human beings who make mistakes, and are, at worst, not worthy of your service.

Of the four pillars of heroic service, the fourth is the toughest to commit to and consistently practice. It is also the most liberating and empowering of the four. Again, that counter-intuitive paradox raises its head. In all three of the foregoing practice pillars, we are the noble knights of the Order of Heroic Service Providers. In our tireless crusade to help others with the head, heart and hands of desire, intent and action, we deliver value in our performance of the Platinum Rule and in doing good turns daily for all whom we serve. *Can you hear the trumpet fanfare and violins rising as we ride into the sunset?*

The fourth pillar is the reality check that allows us to keep our sanity and move forward in a material world with an ever-increasing focus on "What's in it for me?" — bling, power, money and stuff. The modern world is characterized by phrases such as, "I'm going to get mine before you get yours" and "He who dies with the most toys wins the game." I'm confident that if you are a person who holds these beliefs and values, a) you never purchased this book; b) you returned it partially read to the person who shared it with you, pitying them for their naiveté and simplemindedness; or c) someone gave you this book and your pet parrot is enjoying reading it in the bottom of its cage.

The Liberating Power of Forgiveness

I firmly believe that most people do not understand what forgiveness is, how its maximum liberating power is used as a tool, and how it becomes more effective when used proactively instead of reactively, as is most often the case when one seeks forgiveness as an act of contrition through apology.

"Don't let people take up space in your head without paying rent." This is exactly the power that forgiveness provides, as it emboldens and legitimately empowers us to evict those relationships from our conscious minds for whatever act of commission or omission may have been committed. Forgiveness is the positive pole of having been wronged, while its destructive polar opposite is revenge.

"Sticks and stones may break my bones, but words will never hurt me." I don't know the moron to whom this statement deserves attribution, but they are dead, flat-out wrong. Break bones, no. Destroy lives, scar psyches, cause wars and lawsuits and divorces and feuds and riots...absolutely, every day throughout recorded history. Many times, and more often than we think, words are misused and misunderstood, resulting in pain for another person.

Beyond words, there are also actions, or a lack of action, that are equally, if not more, destructive in relationships. Hate, injustice, murder, adultery, deceit — you make up your own list — make us feel hurt, betrayed, dismayed or outraged. The key to letting go of these feelings, regardless of the source, is **complete forgiveness, whether or not our forgiveness is sought by the offending party.**

Courage to Acknowledge Forgiveness

Now this is where I deviate from most conventional wisdom, in that I believe it is important to advise the other person that you are forgiving them, and for which specific action or inaction. Again, this goes back to the basic fundamental truth in open, honest and direct communication. Most people choose to stew in silence when wronged, and then, after some point in time, forgive the person who wronged them. In a lot of cases, people even choose never to forgive, but instead devise grand schemes of revenge that control their thoughts and actions moving forward.

I believe in directly confronting the individual who has wronged you, telling them not only the reason for the forgiveness, but the personal value forgiveness has in liberating you from the pain or negativity of the situation. In so doing, one of three positive outcomes result.

The first — and the one I have found is most common — is that the other person is genuinely unaware an offense has occurred, and will not only accept responsibility for their action and offer an apology, but also seek to perform an act of contrition to balance the scales of the relationship; or...

The other party chooses to disagree with your perception of the situation and puts forth their own beliefs and understanding, and you then have the option to weigh and judge the situation from the other person's point of view. And, believe it or not, as human beings, we may have actually misunderstood, misinterpreted, or misspoken ourselves and now have the ability to acknowledge this, seek forgiveness, and take steps to reaffirm our relationship and move forward; or...

Lastly, the other party for whatever reason may maintain a completely different point of view, and their actions (or inactions) continue to remain out of alignment with your core values, beliefs and principles. At this point, you can disengage in the relationship through forgiveness, forever relieving yourself of the burden of the wrong.

Again, the power of this pillar lies in the action of giving and granting forgiveness even before it is requested. Many people, even knowing they are wrong, lack the character and ability to admit their shortcomings and seek forgiveness, even at the expense of sacrificing a relationship they cherish. By proactively granting forgiveness, we address this situation head-on — and yes, it does take a level of courage — rather than hiding our hurts behind the façade of silence and plastic smiles. How many relationships — personal, professional or other — could have been saved, rehabilitated and made even stronger through the power of forgiveness? Sadly, we will never know. But we can take personal responsibility to ensure that none of our relationships will fall victim to the cowardice of silent disengagement.

🐟 **Wisdom: Just about any problem in the world can be solved through ten minutes of plain talk.**

The Force Multiplier of Forgetting

Forgiving is but half the equation. The true force multiplier is forgetting. Much like energy follows focus, what we focus on expands. If we continually focus on the event to which we gave forgiveness, we run the risk of never venturing into a similar relationship for fear we will be wounded or betrayed in the same manner, or worse. The ability to forget allows us to move forward with the benefit and knowledge of the experience to avoid making the same mistake again, allowing us to seek relationships with the missing, while avoiding those that are toxic.

There is another key benefit to forgetting, and that is, believe it or not, that people and organizations do actually change over time through experience (successes and failures), knowledge (heightened awareness to shortcomings and destructive behaviors) and growth, allowing us the chance to re-engage at some point with someone or with an organization that has, in fact, turned over a new leaf, and whom we would choose to serve as a result.

Not forgetting is like continuing to wear a cast on a broken limb even after it is healed, to remind us of the pain we experienced when we fell out of the tree, preventing us from climbing anything ever again. A great way to be on guard and check yourself for an "unforgetting" attitude is if you hear yourself saying, "I'll never make *that* mistake again."

It is almost impossible to forget completely. After all, without knowledge of our mistakes, we are certainly doomed to repeat them. The focus here on forgetting is to intentionally stop dwelling on the pain of the past so that we are free to experience the joy of the future. Take the lesson from the experience, then let go through the powerful act of forgiveness, which empowers us with the freedom to completely forget, should we so choose. Bottom line: Stop and check not only your forgiveness level, but your forgetting meter, as well.

The other power of forgetting, or not dwelling on the past, is that it frees the finite resource of time to be invested in thoughts, dreams and actions that propel you into the future. You can pursue your limitless success without being sucked into the past of grudges, recrimination and destructive acts of revenge. The sweetest revenge is to lead a happy, rewarding and successful life, as defined by you. Revenge is one of the greatest wastes of time and energy, effectively forcing you to continue to be controlled by a past event that can never be undone. Move on. Let it go. You'll be happy and thankful you did.

> 𝕾 **Wisdom: Forgiveness unloads and returns the heavy rocks that others put in our pack.**

Summary of Fourth Pillar: Forgive and Forget

- Don't let people take up space in your head without paying rent.
- Forgive completely, even when forgiveness isn't sought by others.
- Ten minutes of plain talk can solve just about any problem in the world.
- Forgive, forget, move on!
- Forgiveness unloads the rocks put in your pack by other people.

CHAPTER VII:

THE BREAKAWAY

Following the foregoing advice will let you achieve the ultimate goal: the **BREAKAWAY.**

Break away from the herd and become the leader – the hero. Experience the limitless success and joy in the freedom earned through intention and action to be the very best you can be, and not an imitation, reproduction or emulation of anyone. As substantiated throughout history, true heroes survive the shallow flash of fame. They are unique and challenge the status quo not for fame, but to overcome the challenges faced by those whom they serve. Break away, and through action, boldly set the standards by which all other are measured. 2nd place truly is a 1st place loser. Break away, take the lead, and don't waste time looking back to see if the competition is gaining. Break away, and feel the exhilaration in serving others first. The unfettered joy in the breakaway is even more limitless than the selling success of the hero.

It is my sincere hope and desire that you will take the concepts and pillars of heroic service and make them your own. I hope you will take action – now!

The secret to limitless selling success is not in the study, research or preparation, but in taking action to create first-mover advantage. As you act more, you will develop a rhythm, process and, most importantly, discipline to invest your precious finite hours in activities that yield the highest results in the shortest period of time. You have the power. You choose.

You choose to be the hero and set the performance standards by which your peers and competitors will be measured, all by leveraging the four pillars of heroic service:

Always Give First to Earn More

Practice the Platinum Rule

 Do a Good Turn Daily

Forgive and Forget

My sincere wish is that you have a rich, rewarding and purposeful life through the delivery of ever-increasing value in all your relationships as a heroic servant leader.

Now comes the call to action.

Reading words on a page is an action in itself. Processing those words into ideas is, as well. But if you've received any insight or knowledge from this book, I not only thank you, but also challenge you to take the idea you found most intriguing and immediately put it into daily action. I promise, you won't regret it, and you'll be amazed at the transformation in your sales productivity, as well as the increased joy and quality of your personal relationships.

It is my joy to share. And an even greater joy to see people experience limitless success through the application of these ideas in becoming heroes to others.

This brings us to the end of our road together. I thank you for investing your most precious, priceless resource: time. I trust I've been a good steward of your time, as my measure of success is providing you with tangible returns on your investment.

To your sales success!

WISDOMS

Limitless success is achieved through serving others heroically.
(Page 1)

Attaining limitless success is achieved through intentionally adopting and living the true persona of the ultimate service provider: "the servant."
(Page 2)

The servant <u>earns</u> from a position of power, while the slave is <u>given</u> from a position of submission.
(Page 3)

The hero (or heroes) is an individual (or group) who performs a service for another in a manner that establishes the measure by which all others are measured.
(Page 4)

Heroes endure from generation to generation, while celebrities fade and are soon forgotten.
(Page 5)

Perfection is unattainable. Nevertheless, it is a worthy pursuit as it results in excellence.
(Page 7)

Referrals are free. References must be asked for.
(Page 9)

The Three Keys of Heroic Service Success: Desire, Intent and Action.
(Page 10)

Do something. Anything. Even doing something poorly is more rewarding than doing nothing at all.
(Page 12)

We must be willing to fearlessly give to earn without considering what's in it for us.
(Page 19)

Give a little to earn a lot.
(Page 23)

Do unto others as they want to be done unto.
(Page 26)

A clever man is known by the answers he gives. A wise man is known by the questions he asks.
(Page 35)

People and enterprises that are externally focused on helping and serving others first will explode with success and growth, while those that focus internally on self will implode and limp along to ultimate failure.
(Page 38)

Showing up is half the battle.
(Page 40)

It is the value of taking action, not the value of the act, which counts.
(Page 42)

Focus on the money value of time, and invest your time wisely in activities that yield the highest reward for the time invested.
(Page 44)

Better than the brilliant thought is bold action upon a less-than-perfect thought.
(Page 44)

Thoughts, ideas and words without acts and deeds are but dust in the wind.
(Page 48)

Just about any problem in the world can be solved through ten minutes of plain talk.
(Page 54)

Forgiveness unloads and returns the heavy rocks that others put in our pack.
(Page 54)

I Will Do More

I will do more than belong
*I will **Participate**.*

I will do more than care
*I will **Help**.*

I will do more than believe
*I will **Practice**.*

I will do more than be fair
*I will be **Kind**.*

I will do more than forgive
*I will **Love**.*

I will do more than earn
*I will **Enrich**.*

I will do more than teach
*I will **Serve**.*

I will do more than live
*I will **Grow**.*

I will do more than be friendly
*I will be a **Friend**.*

Think and pray on this
*and then **Act**.*

ACKNOWLEDGEMENTS AND IN MEMORIAM

Writing this book has been a career-long effort in research, observation, experience and preparation, but its creation would have been impossible without a host of special people, beginning with William and Georgia Ann, my parents, whose patience and love is immeasurable.

To my hero, Matt, Semper Fi!

A huge thank you to the countless hours of review, edits, creative design and production coordination with my friends and colleagues, Sydney, Sarah and Leslie.

A special thank you to Tiffany and her untold talent in taking the writer's rough planks and crafting the seamless beams.

To Jon, for encouraging me through his leadership as a successful author himself.

And to all my friends and professional colleagues that kept me accountable with the caring question, *When's the book going to be done?*

Words fail to express my appreciation for the unceasing patience, support, creativity, invaluable counsel, laughter and unfailing love of my beautiful bride of 25 years, Patricia.

In closing, it was my best friend, Steve Harden, and his wife, Becky, who pushed to make this book a reality. On my birthday in 2008, Steve and Becky bought me a round-trip ticket and gave me the keys to their mountain cabin outside Sandia, New Mexico, with a direct instructive from Steve: *You've got to write a book. Not for you, but for those that will be empowered by your words. So here's the ticket, here's the keys, and you've got the cabin for a week. Get it done.* I choose not to live in a world filled with regrets of *woulda, shoulda,* or *coulda.* But I missed the deadline. And now that the book is finally done, Steve has already gone on ahead. I trust he knows the hero was him, not me.

<u>Notes</u>

<u>Notes</u>